# KHAJURAHO

# KHAJURAHO

PHOTOGRAPHS BY RAGHU RAI
TEXT BY LOUIS FRÉDÉRIC

LAURENCE KING

THE PHOTOGRAPHER WOULD LIKE TO THANK
MR. C. JOSHI, DIRECTOR GENERAL, ARCHAEOLOGICAL SURVEY OF INDIA
AND THE LATE MR BALWANT SINGH, FORMER PRINCE OF KHAJURAHO.

PHOTOCREDITS
THE PHOTOGRAPHS (PAGES 155-56) ARE BY RAJA DIN DIYAL (1844-1910), OFFICIAL PHOTOGRAPHER
TO THE NIZAM OF HYDERABAD AND THE MOST DISTINGUISHED NINETEENTH-CENTURY INDIAN
PHOTOGRAPHER. THE PHOTOGRAPH OF VAHARA (PAGE 156, BELOW RIGHT) WAS TAKEN DURING THE
ARCHAEOLOGICAL SURVEY CARRIED OUT IN THE 1870S. THE PENCIL-AND-WASH DRAWINGS
ON PAGES 154 AND 157 ARE BY AN ARMY OFFICER, C. 1850.
MAP (PAGE 158) BY JUDITH CHRISTIE

*PAGE 2:* NEVER HAVING BEEN HUNTED, BOTH ANIMALS AND BIRDS ARE TAME AND ENJOY THE COMPANY OF MEN AND GODS. HERE A RED-HEADED CRANE SEEMS TO BE BEGGING THE VILLAGER FOR A FEW GRAINS OF CORN. FEEDING THE ANIMALS IS CONSIDERED TO BE MAKING AN OFFERING TO THE GODS. *PAGE 6-7:* HUMAN DWELLINGS APPEAR VERY HUMBLE COMPARED TO THE MAJESTY OF A TEMPLE; BUT THE TEMPLE IS ETERNAL, LIKE THE GODS WHO INHABIT IT, UNBORN THEREFORE NOT MORTAL, WHILE THE PEASANTS' DWELLINGS, LIKE EVERYTHING BORN, ARE DOOMED TO DISAPPEAR ONE DAY. ALTHOUGH THE TEMPLE IS NO LONGER IN WORSHIP AND ITS DOOR IS CLOSED, IT STILL BETOKENS THE PRESENCE OF THE DIVINITY. THE CHILDREN PLAYING IN FRONT OF THE PORCH FEEL SECURE AND THEIR PARENTS CAN GO ABOUT THEIR WORK UNTROUBLED. *PAGE 8:* VILLAGE WOMEN VISITING THE TEMPLES. THEIR MOST BEAUTIFUL SARIS AND ALL THEIR JEWELS ARE WORN FOR THE OCCASION. *PAGES 10-11:* THE STRANGE SILHOUETTE OF THE SMALL, SOLITARY TEMPLE OF JAVARI RISES IN THE MIDDLE OF THE FIELDS AMID HUGE SANDSTONE ROCKS FROM WHICH THE STONES OF THE SANCTUARIES WERE EXTRACTED. BIRDS TAKE TURNS TO PERCH THERE LIKE WATCHFUL SENTRIES OF THE GODS.

# P R E F A C E

*I first visited Khajuraho in 1936. It was on the occasion known as Holi, the spring festival during which the small annual fair called the Mela is held. Canvas-covered booths surrounded the temples and a gaudy crowd vied with the crowd of celestial beings inhabiting the facades. No foreign visitors were to be seen in this place which the Murray Guide advised one not to visit, for reasons of decency. But for the local villagers, Khajuraho remained a sacred and magical place. Sometimes a modern Indian in western dress from the Forestry Department would appear, furtively contemplating the erotic scenes, torn between puritanical guilt and pride in a forgotten heritage.*

*Subsequently I stayed at Khajuraho for long periods with Raymond Burnier, a Swiss photographer in the Indian Archeological Service, who had fallen in passionate and sensual love with the Apsaras, the celestial nymphs. He was trying to capture their conspiring glances and equivocal smiles. Camping near the temples, we endeavoured for weeks, on shaky scaffolding in the burning sun, to clean the gods and goddesses and extricate them from the earth and wasps' nests in which they were embedded. We even tried smearing some of the statues with vegetable oil, to make their skin softer and ensure its preservation, as recommended by the ancient texts. For this we were strongly reproved, as the traces are still visible; but we could not however inflict this beauty treatment on the thousands of statues arranged in closely-packed tiered rows on the temple facades and in their most secret recesses.*

*I was already acquainted with the primitive art of Konarak and the more refined art of Bhuvaneshvar. Yet Khajuraho remains for me the pinnacle of sculptural art because of its balance between stylization and realism, which gives surprising life – both ceremonial and sensual – to the characters, and which makes each statue a unique being resembling no other in its beauty, its glances and smiles. The sculptures are not the invention of an inspired artist, but the perception of the existence of indiscernible beings: the skilful craftsman traced a magic diagram to define their proportions before drawing forth from the stone the image of the divinity concealed within. In an ancient Dravidian poem, the Manimekhalai, a sculpted genie on a temple pillar explains the mysterious presence one feels in the statues: "When Maya, the heavenly architect, after keeping a long watch on me, sculpted this statue in my image, the likeness was so great that I felt obliged to inhabit it."*

*According to Hindu philosophy, erotic ecstasy is the image of the mystical union, of the infinite voluptuousness attained when the individual spirit unites with the universal spirit. In the Chhandogya Upanishad (4.3.21) it is written that "just as, in the embrace of the one he loves, a man forgets the whole world, and everything that is inside him is outside, so, in union with the omniscient being, he no longer perceives anything, within or without." This is the message that is endlessly echoed by the erotic sculptures of the temples.*

*As an unexpected consequence of the passion of a young Swiss archeologist whose photographs decorated Jawaharlal Nehru's office, Khajuraho has become a tourist spot, complete with airport and hotels. It attracts crowds whose tactless gaze disturbs the love of gods and goddesses. Fortunately, there also come new disciples, like the authors of this book. Here, they reveal the mystery of a sublime and holy place to those who may never have the privilege of visiting it.*

*Alain Daniélou*
*Le Labyrinthe, June 1990*

# T H E   V I L L A G E

he barbaric-sounding name of this small village in central India suggests a forgotten place, cut off from the world and hidden in some impenetrable jungle, where strange cults are practised. It is, however, just the popular name for a very ancient holy city, Kharjuravahataka, the city of date palms. According to one tradition, it was so named because the gates were adorned with two gilded images of the tree. A more probable reason is that, in former times, date palms grew profusely in the surrounding country.

Very few are left today, as the Indians have little taste for dates and have cut down the trees for timber or firewood. The surrounding area is relatively dry and lightly populated, only becoming fertile after the monsoon rains. Situated in the heart of the province of Madhya Pradesh (the middle country), the region of Bundelkhand in which Khajuraho lies is a rocky plateau of fairly low altitude (about 300 metres) forming a sort of transition between the Vindhya mountains and the River Ganges. The soil, which is either granitic or sandy, is unfit for cultivation except in some areas where the peasants have made sparse fields of corn and barley. Herds of cattle and goats subsist by grazing on the bushes which cover the ground, interspersed with some green pastures where the roots of the trees stretch deep down into the cracks of the earth in search of water.

Most of the time, particularly before the monsoon, the region looks desolate, mercilessly dominated by the sun. The villages seem to wake from their torpor only after the rains. The men set to work in the fields and the children gather together the herds. The women bathe in the replenished Ninora Tal, the great lake, or in the now roaring waters of the river Khudar and then don their most beautiful saris and go to the temple to thank the divinity for this gift from heaven.

The region must once have been much more fertile. Travellers of ancient times speak of three lakes which supplied water to the city: the Ninora Tal, near the old village, the Sib Sagar, between the great temples, and an artificial pool to the north of these. The Chinese voyager Xuanzang, who appears to have visited the site in 601, tells us that this region of Chi-Chi-To (a transcription of the Sanskrit Jejakabhukti, the old name for Bundelkhand), then famous for its fertility, was favoured by numerous scholars and monks

THE STEPS OF THE GHATS, STAIRCASES LEADING DOWN TO THE WATER,

HAVE OFTEN BEEN REPAIRED THROUGHOUT THE CENTURIES, SOMETIMES EVEN WITH STONES TAKEN

FROM THE RUINED TEMPLES. SOME GEESE HESITATE TO GO DOWN

AND PECK THE GRAINS OF CORN SCATTERED FOR THEM, INTRIGUED BY THE SARIS LEFT

ON THE STEPS BY THE BATHING WOMEN.

from every part of India. Much later, in 1335, the Moroccan traveller and chronicler Ibn Batuta rediscovered with amazement the city which he named Kajurra. Although already on the decline, it still harboured many Hindu and Jain ascetics and even some Muslims. When Islam became dominant over the whole of northern India, Khajuraho fell into oblivion, burying itself in the depths of the jungle for fear that some iconoclastic invader might plunder its sanctuaries. Its proud rajahs kept their heads bowed low and managed to survive, in poverty, entrenched in their nearby fortresses at Kalanjar and Mahoba. Even their much-reduced realm was coveted by the sultans of Delhi as well as by Sher Shah the Afghan and the Great Mogul Akbar. Gradually the jungle encroached upon Khajuraho, the earth partially covered and concealed its temples, and tropical storms destroyed the abandoned palaces and mud-and-wood houses that were never to be rebuilt. Only a few peasants born in this hostile country struggled to survive, periodically rebuilding their huts of adobe and cow dung, and life carried on in a small village, all that remained of a forgotten city which was once rich and prosperous.

It was in the 1830s that intrepid English hunters, braving the hazards of the jungle in search of tigers, were astounded to discover the existence of a group of temples in the heart of the unknown. Captivated by their beauty, they informed the department of archaeology. The government sent out archaeologists such as Alexander Cunningham and James Fergusson to study the site. But it was only after 1906 that a serious attempt was made to disengage the ruins from the overgrown bush which hid them from view. Khajuraho then slowly began to come back to life, and the lost village regained some of its importance.

When India became independent in 1947, the new government, having solved its immediate political problems, endeavoured to turn the whole group of temples into a tourist site, building roads, an airfield and a new village for all those attracted by the revival of Khajuraho. Trees were planted, a museum established, hotels were built and the shores of the lake strengthened. The first visitors were Indians. Vast numbers of eternal travellers, forever seeking holy places to venerate in order to acquire merit, came to obtain an auspicious view (*darshan*) of the sacred spot, and also to convince themselves of India's eternity. They passed through, or stopped in the new village for a day, a week, sometimes a few months. Thus, modern life arrived, with the din of motorcycles and back-firing lorries, resounding loudspeakers, the shouts of itinerant vendors, the unwonted glare of pink and green neon lights, and music from the theatres installed to entertain the tourists. The silence which had reigned for centuries in Khajuraho was suddenly replaced by the modern cacophony of nearly every Indian village, the jumbled noises of transistors and traffic, the throbbing of aircraft and hooting of coaches. The latter however disturb the natural tranquillity of the place for only a few hours. Planes and coaches regurgitate their loads of tourists who, after a brief tour and a meal, rapidly get in again, hastening to return to their air-conditioned hotels in Agra or Delhi.

Apart from the temples and the village, there is, in fact, nothing to see other than a chaotic landscape, broken by ravines and covered with dust under a brilliant white sky, a landscape that is burning hot throughout most of the year and impracticable during the monsoon. The temples, whose lofty outline was once reflected in the waters of the lakes, now stand isolated in the middle of lawns that are maintained with difficulty. On good rainy days these form an emerald setting for the golden stone of the sanctuaries, and frogs appear from nowhere, jumping and croaking with joy. But drought soon replaces the abundance of the rainy season, and the mud on the paths turns to dust. The frogs disappear, and only the ever-present, grey-headed crows remain, apparently never troubled by the heat. Perched on high, they observe the slightest movements of humans and animals.

Now water is only found in the wells - either ancient, decorated like the temples, with a spiral ramp leading down to the bottom, or more modern, with concrete curb stones, creaking pulleys, and petrol-driven pumps. These form the centre of village life: in the evening, groups of women gather around them to gossip while the men rest at the foot of a banyan tree, weary after the day's labour. Squatting in a circle, the men smoke and dream while waiting for the chapatis which will whet their appetite for the evening meal. The small shopkeepers have shut their stalls, the craftsmen have closed the workshops where they have been tooling silver bracelets and rings throughout the day. This is the hour known as *goras*, the time when the cows return to the byre along the dusty paths in the golden twilight. Then the village gently prepares for night, which in these latitudes falls very quickly, wrapping in a dark shroud of peace houses and temples, men and gods. Day after day, life continues at the same rhythm, calm and slow, based on resignation and communion with nature. At daybreak all the villagers, after washing briefly, go to the temple to make their devotions to their favourite divinity, Shiva or Vishnu. Thus sanctified, with a red or black spot of *tilaka* on their foreheads, they go about their work as if yesterday never existed and tomorrow will never be; for the whole of India lives in an eternal present.

Looking at the villages and temples of Khajuraho, one finds it hard to imagine that there was once a time when an impressive walled city stood here. Gone are the magnificent palaces and houses, the streets bustling with brahmins and Jain priests, horsemen and merchants, and the colourful processions and ceremonies which took place continuously among the eighty-odd temples dedicated to every imaginable divinity of the then triumphant Hindu religion. It must have been fascinating to behold the crowd of ascetics, beggars, brahmins, rajahs mounted on elephants, resplendent officers, and the endless train of courtiers and monks of every kind who followed them. The palaces built of earth and wood were decorated, the temples brightly coloured. Today Khajuraho looks like any village in central India. Though the ancient village still retains its ancestral appearance, at least for the present, the concrete buildings and electric wires of the new village leave little scope for the imagination.

It is not known exactly when Kharjuravahataka, the holy city of the rajahs of the Rajput Chandella dynasty, was founded. Tradition holds that these rulers were descended from the mythical sage Chandratreya, himself born of the moon. A legend relates that Hemavati, daughter of the great Brahmin of Varanasi, was seduced by this demi-god while bathing in lake Rati. She afterwards gave birth to the first Chandella sovereign, Nannuka. This must have happened at the very beginning of the tenth century. In fact the Chandella were local noblemen, probably paying allegiance to the great Pratihara dynasty which had gained supremacy in the north of India after the fall of the Gupta empire. They belonged to one of the thirty-six Rajput clans, the "sons of kings" of diverse origins assimilated to the warrior caste (Kshatriya) because of their valour in combat. Proud of their divine origin, they stood as fierce defenders of Hinduism against the Muslim advance. But like the feudal lords of the past in Europe, these noblemen found their greatest pleasure in hunting and warfare. Consequently they exhausted each other in endless fighting which served as a pretext to display their courage more than a means to conquer territory. Incapable of uniting when faced with an aggressor, they finally yielded although they never surrendered, often preferring death to the shame of defeat.

Nothing is known about Nannuka, the founder of the Chandella dynasty. One of his sons, Jayashakti (or Jejaka) gave his name to the land which he ruled, Jejakabhukti, and probably established his capital at Kharjuravahataka or thereabouts. His sons succeeded him and gradually enlarged their possessions through interminable wars with other rajahs. It was probably one of his grandsons, Yashovarman, who took advantage of the weakening and final defeat of the last Pratiharas by the Rashtrakuta (a Hindu dynasty in the west of the Dekkan) and secured his position by destroying the power of his neighbours and launching great offensives in order to carve himself a kingdom worthy of his valour. After conquering the rock of Kalanjar he built a formidable fortress there to protect his capital. Upon receiving from King

Devapala of Pratihara a sculpture of Vishnu reputedly from Tibet, he had a magnificent temple built to the god, using his second name, Lakshmana. It was perhaps Yashovarman's son Dhanga (c. 954-1002) who consecrated it in the year of his accession to the throne; this was the case according to an inscription of 49 verses composed by the poet Madhava, dated year 1011 of the Vikrama era, which was found in the vicinity. This sovereign continued to pursue his father's wars of conquest and prestige and succeeded in ensuring the independence of his kingdom. With the spoils collected he built a large number of temples at Khajuraho, although he had transferred his capital to Kalanjar. He was a fervent worshipper of Shiva and appears to have finally committed suicide (at the age of a hundred!) by drowning himself in the waters at the confluence of the Ganges and the Yamuna, "entering into beatitude, closing his eyes, setting his mind on Rudra and murmuring prayers."

Little is known about his son Ganda other than the fact that he reigned until 1019. One of his noblemen, Kokkala, of the Garhaspatya family, built a temple to Shiva, the Vaidyanatha, and an unknown poet had the following inscription engraved on it: "I worship the adorable coil of matted hair carried by the beautiful Vaidyanatha, which is irradiated by the expanding terrible hoods of a multitude of hissing broad serpents; marked with the half-moon which is excessively shining, more brilliantly than the sun; and yellowish, when in contact with the line of flames of the fire issuing forth from his tremulous eyes." (*Epigr. Ind.*, I, 150)

Even in the years before Dhanga's suicide, the Turkish sultan Mahmud of Ghazni was making devastating annual raids into India with the aim of looting the riches of the cities and temples. On at least one occasion his troops had even beaten Dhanga's army, but they had not reached Khajuraho yet. During the reign of Vidyadhara (1019-1022), Mahmud of Ghazni launched another great offensive. Vidyadhara was a warrior in the great Rajput tradition, and he put up fierce resistance. He fought the invaders on the banks of the Ganges with an army of 145,000 infantry, 36,000 cavalry and 390 military elephants. But at nightfall he retired from the battlefield, leaving his camp prey for Mahmud to ransack. The Turk took full advantage of the opportunity. Vidyadhara then went to Kanauj, which had surrendered to the Muslims earlier.

In 1022 Mahmud returned to the charge, this time making a direct attack on the fortresses of Gwalior and Kalanjar. Gwalior soon yielded and Vidyadhara took refuge at Kalanjar, but as this fort was on the verge of capitulating due to lack of water, Vidyadhara chose to buy peace with the Muslims, who withdrew without pillaging the city. To reward Vidyadhara for showering him with gold, Mahmud made him governor of all the fortresses in the region, at little expense to himself since he could not occupy them and was in haste to return to Ghazni. Jejakabhukti, not having been sacked, was still a rich kingdom, and Vidyadhara was able to continue embellishing his religous city of Khajuraho with new temples. He is generally thought to have built, among other sanctuaries, the Kandariya Mahadeo.

The truce established by the Rajput with Mahmud of Ghanzi, probably reinforced by the payment of tribute by the Chandellas to Mahmud, enabled Vidyadhara to combat other Hindu rulers such as the Paramaras and the Kalachuris. The latter were temporarily defeated by his son Vijayapala (1022-1049). His successors fought incessantly to preserve their independence. Madanavarman, who reigned from 1129 to 1163, succeeded in enlarging the Chandella territories to such an extent that, in his inscriptions, he prides himself on controlling the regions of Bhilsa (site of the famous Buddhist stupa of Sanchi), Mau, in the modern district of Jhansi, Ajaigarh, Mahoba and Kalanjar, in addition to the areas of Chhattarpur and of course Khajuraho. It is uncertain whether the latter remained his capital, for he seems to have settled in Mahoba or Kalanjar.

However Khajuraho continued to be the supreme holy city of the Chandellas, the one created by the founder of their dynasty. When attacked by the Chalukya kings of Gujarat, towards the end of his reign, Madanavarman was forced to give back the Bhilsa district. His son Paramardi (also known as Parmal), who reigned between 1165 and 1201, was able to conserve the Chandella patrimony, and to reconquer the Bhilsa territory, probably a short time after 1173. But in about 1182 he was in turn defeated by King Prithiviraja III of the Chauhan who invaded the Jejakabhukti territory and withdrew immediately after exacting tribute from the Chandellas. In 1202 the sultan of Delhi, Qutb ud-Din Aibak, laid siege to Kalanjar, the Chandella fortress defending the site of Khajuraho. Paramardi agreed to pay the sultan a large indemnity and to give him elephants, but his minister Ajayadeva, outraged by the rajah's attitude, killed him and resumed war with the Muslims. Besieged in Kalanjar, Ajayadeva was forced to surrender because of the lack of water in the fort. Qutb ud-Din plundered the fortress and seized the Chandellas' other capital, Mahoba, where he installed a Muslim governor, Hazabdar ud-Din Hassan Arnal. This insane struggle is recounted in the *Alha Cycle*, a collection of chivalrous narratives composed by the poet Jaganayaka in the thirteenth century under the title *Alhakhand*. The heroic exploits of the wars are still sung about today in the villages of Bundelkhand.

Paramardi's son and successor, Trailokyavarman, succeeded in regaining the fortress and Mahoba, shortly before 1205. At the same time he further increased his possessions at the expense of other Hindu rajahs. He was repeatedly attacked and pillaged by the troops of Malik Nusrat ud-din

Tayasai, a general of the sultan of Delhi Iltutmish, although he did not lose any of his territories. Trailokyavarman's successors appear to have retained their possessions at the cost of perpetual wars against either the sultans of Delhi, or the other Hindu sovereigns. However, in 1310 Sultan Ala ud-Din Khalji assembled considerable armies for the purpose of making profitable looting operations. He invaded Jejakabhukti. The Chandella rajahs were unable to resist: Kalanjar was taken and Khajuraho ravaged, its temples partially destroyed. Some were spared, as Ala ud-Din Khalji's soldiers were aiming not to uproot Hinduism but to lay hands on the treasures of the temples. The Chandellas no doubt resisted desperately. During the battles the city of Khajuraho was burnt down, its palaces destroyed and the ramparts demolished. Yet the invaders spared some of the temples, probably because, once again, the last Chandellas paid the Muslims to leave. However, nothing more is known of the sovereigns of this dynasty after Viravarman II, whose last attested date is 1315.

After the annihilation of their religious capital and the occupation of Mahoba and Kalanjar, the Chandellas lost all historical importance and their rajahs became mere village chiefs. Yet it was this obscurity which saved the site of Khajuraho. Since the Chandellas no longer represented a danger to the conquering sultans and the city held no more treasures to arouse their greed, they were simply forgotten. The village heads, descendants of the proud Rajputs who had erected the temples, were now reduced to a bare living and could no longer raise troops and wage war, still less rebuild the ruins of the dilapidated sanctuaries. So they let the jungle overrun the site, now deserted by the faithful, and wild animals made their lairs in the temples. The lakes which had once helped to bring prosperity to the city disappeared, their shores no longer maintained.

This was the state in which Khajuraho was rediscovered, first by Ibn Batuta who found it very poor, although he notes that in about 1335 many ascetics still dwelt around the sacred lake. Five centuries later, the site was again discovered, by other foreigners. It had been gradually abandoned by the holy men for whom the temples, once desecrated, were no longer inhabited by the gods. The Indians had forgotten that this place, once regarded as one of the holiest in India, a *tirtha* frequented by sages of every religion, had been a religous capital almost as prestigious as Varanasi, and the seat of a dynasty which during the tenth and eleventh centuries was one of the most powerful in Hindu India. There only remain some twenty or twenty-five temples, impassive observers of the passing of time and the suffering of men, whose magnificent ornamentation bears witness to the fervour of the rulers responsible for their creation.

The banks of the Khajuraho lake are always crowded with people who come to bathe or to wash their linen on steps worn away by the centuries. The women bathe dressed in their saris, the wet material clinging to their sculptural figures as they emerge from the water. This sight must have inspired many an artist, an ephemeral vision soon to be dissipated by the sun which dries the veils in a few minutes. *PAGES 20-21:* On the road leading to Khajuraho, better adapted to the herds of goats and buffalo than to cars, there are still some hill-top residences of maharajahs who were at the height of their power in the eighteenth century and built lavish palaces in the Indo-Mughal style of the period. *PAGES 22-23:* At sundown, when the cool of evening brings calm to the village and temples, women return from the fields and the well, balancing pitchers on their heads and accompanying the cattle back to the cowshed. This is the hour of rest, of evening prayer and of peace regained.

T AKING A DIP IN THE WATER IS A BLESSING IN THE HEAT, AND THE CHILDREN ENJOY IT AS MUCH AS
THEIR MOTHERS, WHO TAKE THE OPPORTUNITY TO WASH THEM AT THE SAME TIME. THE MANY GLASS
BRACELETS WORN PERMANENTLY BY THE WOMEN GENERALLY COME FROM EUROPE.

In the new village of Khajuraho just as in the ancient one, life goes on in the street rather than inside the houses. There people talk, work, make their devotions to Shiva in a small domed temple, built recently and whitewashed, and light fires for the evening's cooking, surrounded by hens and buffalo indifferent to the activities of human beings (*ABOVE*). *LEFT:* In the village any excuse is good for meetings and interminable discussions. While waiting for the festivities to begin, men and women rest on the cool stone of the square in front of the temple or spread out newly-washed saris to dry in the shade.

Dressed in red, the mother of the young prince waits patiently while her son, surrounded by friends and relatives, receives instruction from a guru. The group is shaded from the sun by a fine white cotton awning. *pages 32-33:* In the evening of a feast day a village dance is held to the blaring of loudspeakers. The women come dressed in their best but do not seem to enjoy the dancing, finding it too westernized. Nevertheless, they take advantage of this occasion to meet, talking endlessly and, sometimes, laughingly, doing a few pirouettes among themselves, just for fun.

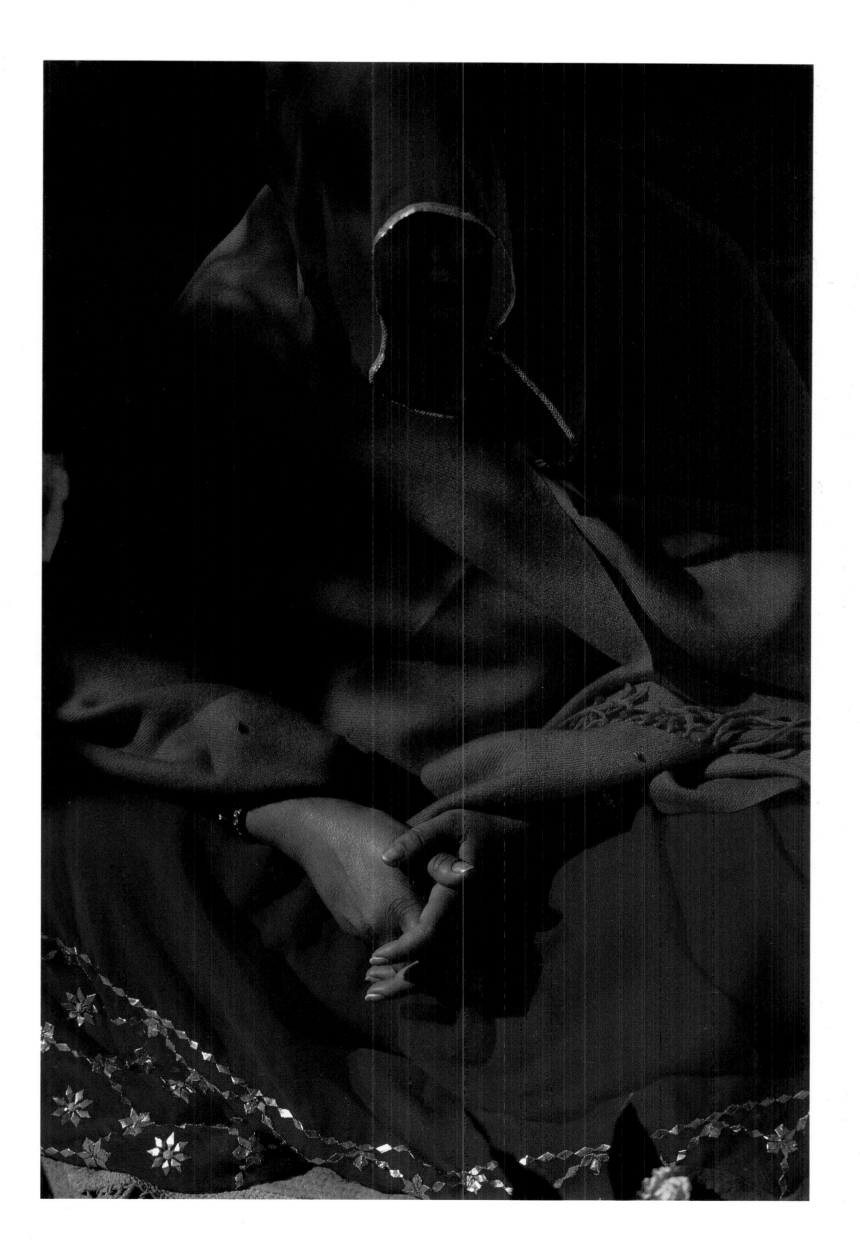

In the open spaces between the temples and in the village square, acrobats and wrestlers demonstrate their talents, watched with admiration by the villagers, who love this type of entertainment. *PAGES 34-35:* In the evening, under the blaze of projectors, with the silhouette of a temple as a back-cloth, troupes of players enact episodes from the *RAMAYANA* or other famous stories that everyone knows by heart. Like the actors symbolizing the divinities, the spectators enter into the realm of the sacred. *PAGES 38-39:* A maharajah with his hunting trophies. Such souvenirs are evidence of past splendour, of a time when the local lord revelled in hunting and war alike. His shimmering costume, nowadays abandoned in favour of drab western suits, is also just a souvenir.

# THE TEMPLES

The traveller arriving by road or by plane from Delhi or Agra is first tempted, or rather encouraged, to rest awhile at one of the newly-built hotels in the modern village, from which point he can glimpse the whorled spires of some of the temples belonging to what is called the western group. In order to facilitate the visit, the temples have been arbitrarily divided into groups which do not correspond at all to the original arrangement of the Chandellas' holy city. The "western" group corresponds to the temples situated near the modern village, while the "eastern" group is at some distance to the east of the ancient one. A few more temples, some ruined structures and piles of debris are found scattered about the surrounding country. The chaotic aspect of the disposition of the temples is due to the disappearance of a large number of them, and also to their being constructed around sacred lakes of which only an indistinct trace can be seen today. The ancient holy city of Khajuraho must however have been designed on a clearly defined plan according to the religious norms governing the foundation and organization of towns, as described in architectural treatises like the *Mayamata*.

Nothing could be left to chance, if the gods were to be favourably disposed towards a new city. First came the choice and consecration of the site, then its orientation was decided with the use of a gnomon. The fertility of the soil was ascertained by sowing different types of seeds on which animals had to tread: "In this way, the site shall be trodden by cows, sanctified by their breath, purified by the joyful lowing of bulls and consecrated by the froth flowing from the mouths of calves; it shall be bathed in cows' urine, made fertile by the saliva that flows as they ruminate and by their trampling feet; it shall be then pervaded with their smell and, finally, consecrated by the ritual sprinkling." (*Mayamata* IV, 5-8a)

There is therefore no doubt that the site had been carefully chosen, ploughed and ritually prepared and that the streets, houses and temples each had their predetermined place in relation to the divinities which presided over their building. The presence of water was a determining factor as it was a sign of life. An examination of the Khajuraho site reveals numerous traces of lakes, ponds and various pools which must have made the area a spot blessed by the gods, a place where life was pleasant in the shade of ancient

ON A DAY OF CELEBRATION, THE WOMEN OF KHAJURAHO AND
THE NEIGHBOURING VILLAGES CROWD ONTO THE STEPS OF THE MATANGESHVARA, EACH HOLDING A
SPOTLESS LOTA. CLIMBING THE STAIRCASE SYMBOLIZES THE ASCENT TOWARDS
A HIGHER SPIRITUAL PLANE, AS DO ALSO THE TIERED TOWERS OF THE LAKSHMANA TEMPLE SEEN
IN THE BACKGROUND.

trees and date palms. The establishment of a capital in this particular place was due primarily to the power suddenly gained by the Chandellas as a result of the decline of the Kanauj empire, and to the consequent arrival of a throng of monks and common people anxious to put themselves under the protection of powerful warriors.

Since Kanauj, now impoverished, could no longer build temples, its artists and craftsmen thronged to the wealthy capital of the Chandellas, to enrich it with their skills and art. With them came brahmins who were versed in the holy writings and knew how to build, decorate and consecrate sanctuaries. Probably other artists – architects, sculptors and painters – like Shri Kana, Satana and Chitanaka whose names remain engraved on the stones, came in great numbers from other parts of India, drawn by the sumptuous reputation of Jejakabhukti. As in mediaeval Europe, corporations of artist-priests travelled the sovereigns' states, settling wherever the rajahs required their services and departing when the money ran out.

Of all this minute organization behind the creation of Khajuraho and its temples, nothing remains except a few "well-preserved ruins". It would therefore be futile to try to study the buildings according to a clearly determined plan. For the visit we have to confine ourselves to the classification into distinct groups which has been imposed. In his book *Indian Architecture,* Percy Brown writes: "The Khajuraho temples do not illustrate a development over a long period of time, for, as shown by inscriptional evidence, they were all erected within the relatively narrow interval of a hundred years, from about A.D. 950 to 1050. They imply therefore a brilliant episode in the history of Indian temple architecture..." In fact, according to recent studies, certain temples may date from the early ninth century and others from the beginning of the twelfth. However, from what is known at present, and in view of the very few inscriptions relating to Khajuraho, it is difficult to assign a more precise date to these monuments. Yet they represent one of the pinnacles of Indian art, both in their perfection of design and construction and in the quality of their decorative sculpture. The majority of the temples have a sharply defined architectural character, akin to the general northern Indian style called Nagara. This peculiar style is the final version of one of the architectural styles which first appeared in the region of Pattadakal at the end of the seventh and the beginning of the eighth centuries then continued with some variations, notably at Bhuvaneshvar in Orissa in the tenth century, and reached its ultimate achievement at Khajuraho.

The visitor is first struck by the fact that the temples are built on high terraces which either isolate them or group them together. This is unusual in India where temples are normally enclosed by walls and built at ground level. Some of these terraces, such as that of the Lakshmana, are edged with balustrades; others are not, either because they never existed or because they were destroyed. Next, one is surprised by their relatively small size, the largest being scarcely thirty metres long and high. They are all constructed of blocks of beige and pinkish fine-grained sandstone from the quarries at Panna, situated some distance away on the banks of the river Ken. The stone was quarried by means of wooden wedges inserted into the rock and moistened so that they would expand. Once transported to the site the split blocks of rock were squared and trimmed, and sometimes even sculpted before being hoisted into place with winches and wooden ramps, then secured without cement, resting on one another simply by their weight. In certain places, however, the architects, having little confidence in the strength of the edifice, bound them together with wrought-iron clamps. Though the technique was sometimes empirical the architects showed themselves to be innovators in many respects. They made the towers hollow in order to reduce their weight, piling series of columned rooms on top of each other. These rooms had no religious use and were completely inaccessible. To strengthen the towers (here called *shikharas*) they devised a whole series of buttresses, each one a smaller version of the central tower, rising in tiers one above the other on each side of the main shikhara. Being constructed on the stable and rigid foundation of the elevated terraces, their walls have not sunk and the bases of the stones have remained horizontal.

It is thanks to these artifices that the Khajuraho monuments have withstood the onslaught of time and the elements. But these results were not obtained spontaneously. A study of the various temples reveals the technical progress which evolved as they were being built. Thus the Jain temple of Adinatha has a simple, curvilinear shikhara whose upward movement is produced solely by the vertical bands on the sides. This relatively small temple, located within the same enclosure as its more perfected neighbour Parshvanatha, represents the Khajuraho style in its initial stage. On the temple dedicated to Vishvanatha situated in the western group one notices the first outline of buttresses: on each side of the tower is a semi-shikhara of exactly the same shape as the main tower, including the final motif. A sanctuary-niche adorns the front of these supports, while on the sides and on every corner there arise other small shikharas (*urushringa*) distinct from the main mass of the tower. The following stage is illustrated by the Jain temple of Parshvanatha, very close to the Adinatha temple. Here a second semi-shikhara (or *anga-shikhara*) is placed against the first, reinforcing its base and replacing the sanctuary-niche. Other anga-shikharas situated on the sides of the first, support it laterally, while the base of the tower is surrounded by more urushringas. The technique becomes progressively more complex, reaching its peak in the great sanctuary of Khajuraho, the Kandariya-Mahadeo. Here four projecting storeys of anga-shikharas support the large central tower, each one diminishing in size and height from the top downwards, with miniature shikharas filling all the receding angles. The whole tower consists of 16 anga-shikharas and 28 urushringas forming a plane with projections which is faithfully repeated inside the sanctuary. The base of the tower is set on a high decorated plinth (*pabhaga*) above which are windows with balconies.

The overall plan of the temples is generally orientated west-east with the main entrance facing the rising sun. The temples are laid out on a linear system, like those of Orissa. The sanctuary tower opens on the east side onto a porch (*antarala*) which communicates with a square, columned hall (*maha-mandapa*), which in turn opens to the outside by a corridor (*ardha-mandapa*) and an entrance hall (*mandapa*) followed by a flight of steps leading to the platform. Each section appended to the sanctuary tower has its own pyramidal roof (usually four-sided) with multiple false floors characterized by horizontal superimposed line gradually diminishing up to the topmost motif, which consists of one, two or three inverted lotus-blossoms topped by a vase (*kalasha*). The shikharas, anga-shikharas and urushringas are always surmounted by a flattened, ribbed cushion (*amalaka* – from the name of the myrobolam fruit which it resembles). This is completed by one, two or three inverted lotus blossoms and a kalasha vase symbolizing the spiritual summit attained by the faithful after ascending through the different stages which lead to a mystical union with the divinity. The shikhara as a whole also represents Mount Meru, in Indian cosmogony the world's axis, on whose slopes dwell the minor divinities presided over by Indra, "king of the gods". In the temples dedicated to Shiva it symbolizes his celestial palace on Mount Kailasa, thought to be situated far to the north beyond the Himalayas.

This simple linear plan quickly evolved, first into a Latin cross with a transept at the point of the sanctuary, then a double cross with two transepts, one at the sanctuary and the other at the mandapa immediately preceding it. The transepts were then given concrete form by means of projecting balconies covered with tilted roofs and windows letting the light directly into the maha-mandapa and the corridor (*pradakshinapatha*) outside the sanctuary itself (*garbha-griha*). The statue or symbol of the principal divinity of the temple was enclosed in almost complete darkness, as required by divine mystery.

The most important temples are of the type known as Panchayatana, with five sanctuaries. At each of the four corners of the platform stands a lesser temple in the shape of a small isolated tower, dedicated to a secondary divinity. Some others have a pavilion either on the same platform or on another placed in front of their entrance. This is reserved for the vehicle (*vahana*) of the god, for example Nandin the white bull for Shiva, or the representation of an *avatar*, such as Varaha the wild boar, for Vishnu.

No two temples are exactly alike, either in their layout, decoration or chosen divinity. As we shall see later, eclecticism seems to have been the rule, together with tolerance: the great Hindu divinities Shiva and Vishnu as well as their Jain counterparts shared the favour of the Chandella sovereigns. The only sanctuaries which stand apart from the others, forming a separate group (though architecturally similar) and enclosed by walls preventing them from being sullied by the external world, are the three Jain temples dedicated to the prophets (*tirthankara*) Adinatha, the first, Parshvanatha and Shantinatha. They scarcely differ from the Brahmanic temples other than in their decoration.

The interiors of the sanctuaries are quite as remarkable as the exteriors. At the base of the great tower, as if hollowed out of it, there is always the Holy of Holies harbouring the statue or symbol of the divinity. Enfolded in darkness, with no opening other than the entrance, and usually square in shape, this represents the cave, the matrix from which all life comes forth. No one is allowed in it except the brahmin appointed to perform the sacrifices. On the threshold of the vestibule leading into it a large crescent-shaped stone marks this entrance, sometimes flanked by two columns or piers decorated with auspicious motifs referring to fecundity, such as the anthropomorphic effigies of the Ganga and Yamuna rivers linked with their symbols, the sea-monster (*makara*) and the tortoise. The faithful must therefore make a detour around the left side of the garbha-griha, keeping the divinity on their right, and proceed clockwise along the corridor of pilgrimage, or pradakshinapatha, reserved for their use. Animated by the spiritual power of the officiating brahmin, the divinity becomes a sort of accumulator of divine energy which flows into the faithful when they touch the outer wall of the sanctuary during the ritual procession. The pradakshinapatha is therefore lit by balconies with small, narrow windows. The temple known (erroneously) as Chitragupta, from the name of a secretary of Yama, king of the dead (it was, in fact, erected to the sun-god Surya), is the only one to have no pradakshinapatha. There the procession takes place around the temple.

The ceilings of the garbha-griha are generally small and often in the form of imitation cupolas with successive overhanging slabs of stone. An exception is the ceiling of the maha-mandapa, the great hall preceding the sanctuary, where the architects made use of empirical expedients adapted according to their fancy. Four solid pillars joined at the top by heavy architraves diminish and divide the vacant space, similarly reducing the surface of the ceiling. Successive rows of stone beams restrict the area overhead to a series of octagons of gradually diminishing size. The final octagon holds the hollow dome-shaped stone which constitutes the vault. This is adorned with a finely-worked pendant and the whole is so elaborately engraved that the underlying structure becomes invisible. A model for this type of ceiling could only have been found in wooden architecture. All the elements, which had to support the massive weight of the pyramidal roof, were probably carved and assembled on the ground before being put in place piece by piece at the final stage of building. The same procedure was used for the ceiling of the vestibule of the garbha-griha, and of the ardha-mandapa of the entrance, which sometimes have two ceilings with interior domes on account of their length, for example in the Kandariya Mahadeo and the Lakshmana. There too the architect has placed hollow spaces just above the ceilings in order to reduce the considerable weight of the pyramidal roofs of these appended rooms. The whole is strongly bound together and forms a solid, coherent mass. The projecting balconies marking the transepts at the level of the garbha-griha and the maha-mandapa also serve to relieve the weight, their roofs being supported by columns.

The arrangement of the interior is designed so that the worshipper progresses from the full daylight of the ardha-mandapa, through the dimmer light of the mandapa and maha-mandapa to the half-light of the processional corridor, before finally glimpsing the darkness of the Holy of Holies. In this way he penetrates gradually to the heart of the divine mystery and, by virtue of his presence, ultimately partakes of it.

Before entering, the worshipper walks around the temple with the building on his right. As the temple is mounted on a very high, decorated plinth, he then climbs slowly and sometimes painfully up the steps leading to the threshold of the ineffable.

Situated somewhat apart from the two main groups are a few temples which differ from the general rule. The one dedicated to Vamana, the dwarf-avatar of Vishnu, is very simple, its shikhara having no supporting anga-shikhara. This was probably one of the first to be built on the site. Located nearby is the Javari, a small temple measuring approximately twelve metres by seven, perhaps built by a brahmin. Its mandapa, perched on columns and open on every side, gives it an extremely graceful appearace. The Brahma (actually consecrated to Vishnu) must be even older; it is generally dated around 900. Its undecorated granite base bears a simple sandstone shikhara. Further to the west are two temples clearly distinct from the main group.

These seem to have been among the earliest to be built at Khajuraho. The first consists of the vestiges of the temple known as the Chaunshat Yogini (the 64 women votaries of the goddess Kali) because three sculptures representing servants of the goddess were found on the spot. But whether this was really a temple is not certain. It consists of a high granite platform about 31 by 18 metres surrounded by flights of stairs and must have stood on the edge of a small lake situated to the northeast. Around the platform are arranged 65 very simple small granite sanctuaries each crowned by a rudimentary shikhara, their entrance (originally closed by a wooden door) facing the platform. In the middle of the southwest row rises a sanctuary, or perhaps a cell, slightly higher than the rest. It is impossible to say whether this was the site of a wooden temple or a former palace, or perhaps merely a royal enclosure where meetings or special ceremonies were held. Nothing enables us to establish the date or the nature of the building. However, as it appears older than the other monuments, we are justified in thinking that it belonged to a regional style anterior to the Chandella period. The small temple of Lalguan Mahadeva further to the west, dedicated to Shiva, appears to be a transition between the Chaunsat Yogini and the authentic Chandella temples, being built of granite and sandstone like the Brahma. It is unfortunately in ruins.

In the midst of the jungle about two kilometres to the south, beyond the village of Jatkari and the river Khudar, stands a small temple dedicated to Vishnu, which contrary to the norm, opens to the west. Once part of a large group of temples now no longer existing, its shikharas and niches with round miniature columns indicate a relatively late period, perhaps the end of the eleventh century. It has been named Chaturbhuja on account of the great effigy of Vishnu in the inner sanctuary. The Duladeo temple, located on the bank of the river Khudar and dedicated to Shiva, appears to date from the same period. Its roofing is unfortunately in very bad condition.

Finally we must mention the ruins of a particular temple in the old village, one which must have been magnificent judging from what remains of it. This is the Ghanta, so called because of the bell-flower (*ghanta*) decoration on the pillars. A Jain temple, it must have been at least twice as big as the Parshvanatha which it resembled in style. The round-cut columns of its mandapa supporting capitals with crouching dwarfs (*gana*) have lateral projections on two levels, probably used to hold lamps.

All the temples are elaborately decorated, either with sculptures carved in the round or engraved ornamental designs. Yet this profusion of floral, animal and human motifs never detracts from the general outline of the buildings, which represents and symbolizes both the divine mountain and the gradual ascent to self-fulfilment, the ultimate goal of Hindu philosophy.

Although, apart from the Matangeshvara, practically none of the temples are still consecrated, Hindus flock from every part of India to climb the steps, to pay homage to their ancestors and to admire the skill of architects and sculptors of the past. They never forget that the gods long resided in this place, even though they now seem absent. As both believers and tourists, they honour the gods by wearing their finest clothes. But do they still know what these temples and sculptures represented? Are they really aware of their prestigious past? *PAGES 48-49:* Shiva is still venerated, especially on propitious days. The villagers of Khajuraho and the neighbourhood crowd before the Matangeshvara in order to obtain a Darshan, or auspicious sight, of the divinity whose name is engraved over the entrance. *PAGES 54-55:* Meeting a friend from a nearby village on the bank of the lake is always a pleasure. The girls enjoy bathing together and laugh as they dry their glistening saris in the soothing breeze, not far from a recently restored temple.

THE DIVINITIES, NUMBERING 33 MILLION, ARE EVERYWHERE, AND THE BODY OF VISHNU'S AVATAR, THE WILD BOAR VARAHA, CONTAINS THEM ALL. EACH HAS ITS OWN FUNCTION DIRECTLY RELATED TO HUMAN ACTIVITIES. THESE ARE REPRESENTED ON THE FRIEZES OF THE TEMPLE PLATFORMS: THIS ORGY BEFORE BATTLE IS AIMED AT ENSURING THE VICTORY OF THE PARTICIPANTS. *PAGES 58-59:* THE JAIN TEMPLES OF KHAJURAHO USUALLY HAVE A MORE SOBER APPEARANCE THAN THOSE OF THE BRAHMANIC CULTS, YET THEIR WALLS ARE DECORATED WITH MAGNIFICENT IMAGES OF THE GODS. WORSHIP IS STILL GOING ON IN THESE TEMPLES AND MORE RECENT STRUCTURES HAVE BEEN ADDED WHICH, THOUGH REMINISCENT OF THE CHANDELLA ARCHITECTURE IN GENERAL, FAIL TO EQUAL ITS MAGNIFICENCE.

Every corner of the temple superstructure is furnished with sculptures in high relief, but this profusion never destroys the main outline of the architecture. The protruding corners are embellished with figures of gods and women, while the receding ones have images of chthonic spirits, (naga), symbolizing water and poetry. They can be recognized by their serpentine hoods and hands joined in adoration. *PAGES 62-63:* A griffin is apparently attempting to crush a kneeling man. The exact meaning of this group is unknown, but it probably represents the power of the senses over human nature. A frieze on the base of the adjacent temple depicts cavalry setting off for war. *PAGES 64-65:* In the evening, when the stone, worn away by the elements, shimmers in the last rays of the setting sun, one can sometimes catch a glimpse of the moon from the balcony at the temple entrance.

SOME TEMPLES HAVE WITHSTOOD THE TEST OF TIME AND, BEING WELL RESTORED, STILL RISE IN ALL THEIR MAJESTY. OTHERS LIKE THE CHAUNSAT YOGINI, BUILT OF GRANITE, ARE TOO DAMAGED FOR THEIR ORIGINAL FORM TO BE RECONSTRUCTED. ARCHAEOLOGISTS STILL ARGUE ABOUT THE VOCATION OF THIS SANCTUARY, ITS CELLS AROUND A COURTYARD CONTRASTING STRANGELY WITH THE PERFECT WHOLE OF THE GREAT KANDARIYA-MAHADEO TEMPLE (*ABOVE*). *LEFT:* ALTHOUGH THE TEMPLES ARE BUILT ON HIGH PLATFORMS THEY MUST NOT BE ON THE SAME LEVEL AS HUMANS, AND ARE THEREFORE RAISED A FEW STEPS HIGHER. HERE THE MANDAPA HOUSING THE COLOSSAL STATUE OF NANDIN, THE WHITE BULL OF SHIVA, IS DECORATED WITH FRIEZES LIKE THE TEMPLES THEMSELVES. IT IS OPEN ON EVERY SIDE, ENABLING THE GOD'S SYMBOL TO SEE THE CREATION AROUND. WOMEN FREQUENTLY PRAY TO IT TO BE GRANTED MANY CHILDREN. *PAGES 68-69:* THROUGH THE OPENINGS OF THE BALCONY AT A TEMPLE ENTRANCE THE PYRAMIDAL FORM OF ANOTHER STRUCTURE CAN BE SEEN. DIVINITIES AND LOVE SCENES ALTERNATE ON THE WALLS. THE SHAFTS OF THE PILLARS ARE ENHANCED WITH SCULPTURES WHICH COME ALIVE IN THE SOFT EVENING LIGHT AND SEEM ABOUT TO SPRING OUT OF THE STONE.

The gods are eternal, but the material from which their images are made is apt to deteriorate, as matter is in constant transmutation. Sometimes, at the foot of the temples, statues lie in the grass, in an attitude of well-earned rest. The god no longer inhabits them and they are abandoned. Refusing to hear their desperate calls for revival, man turns his back on them, seeing only darkness. *PAGES 70-71:* At the bottom of the temple steps a griffin attacks a noble figure. Is this a symbol of the power of carnal desire over human beings, or is it an allegory of the Chandella empire's ability to crush its enemies like a lion destroying a weak, defenceless creature? *PAGES 72-73:* The high pyramidal towers of the Matangeshvara and the Lakshmana appear faintly through the trees as the sun sets on the horizon. Their tall, slender shape and the ramifications of the upper stories blend perfectly with the natural surroundings.

The devotion of the faithful towards their divinities takes various forms. Here someone has placed a banknote among the flowers on a moulding at the top of the steps leading to a temple entrance. Elsewhere a necklace of jasmine and canna flowers bedecks a figure clinging to the neck of Shiva's mount, the bull Nandin. *Pages 76-77:* In the early morning mist and in the golden light of evening, the temples watch over the fortunes of men, the village and the cattle grazing in the fields. Every day, unfailingly, the villagers sweep the courts in honour of the gods. *Pages 78-79:* Wherever it is good, all around the village and right up to the foot of the temples, the soil is cultivated. The sculptures of heavenly spirits on the temple walls seem to watch the meticulously ploughed earth for the germination of the seeds, and to be ready to protect them.

Flowers at the feet of a divinity, a thoughtful expression before the unfathomable mystery of shadows and light in the narrow corridor around the sanctuary. One wonders which is more admirable, the silent devotion or the wondering contemplation of the worshipper. *Pages 84-85:* Worshippers walk around the great effigy of Vahara, the boar avatar of Vishnu, adorned with the thousands of divinities the god embodies in order to safeguard the human race and all earthly beings. The worshippers follow the direction of the sun, praying with clasped hands, in the hope that Vishnu will help them earn eternal life.

# THE SCULPTURES

Although the temples of Khajuraho owe their fame to the many erotic scenes represented there, which scandalized the first European travellers to the site as well as certain Indians ill-acquainted with all the religious philosophies of their country, the sculptured decoration of the Chandella sanctuaries is not restricted to images of this kind. Scenes of battles, dancing, animals fighting, daily activites. representations of divinities and imaginary beasts, floral and vegetable ornaments all occupy the interior and exterior surfaces and the bases of the temples. With very rare exceptions, no undecorated surface exists, yet this in no way harms the general outlines of the architecture. The abundance of decoration is mainly religious in essence. The scenes of battles and military parades no doubt illustrate the martial feats of the Rajputs who commissioned them.

The Chandellas were fervent Hindus but, unlike other Indian sovereigns, they demonstrated extreme tolerance, allowing followers of Shiva and Vishnu to exist side by side with Jain monks. There is a possibility that Buddhist communities also lived in Khajuraho or at least nearby, as some statues of Buddha have been found in the vicinity. We know from an inscription (*A.S.I.* 1929-1930, 166-167) that the rajah Parmal, when making a donation of land to some brahmins in 1179, set aside a part which had belonged to a Buddhist temple.

Though the first Chandella rajahs were mainly followers of the Vishnu cults, some of them had Jain teachers. Most of their successors seem to have belonged to the Shiva cults, although they were also responsible for the building of sanctuaries dedicated to multiple divinites. The sculpted decoration reflects their religious preoccupations. While the Jain temples are devoid of erotic images, the walls of those dedicated to Shiva abound with them. The Jain faith considers that chastity is a form of avoidance of harm (*ahimsa*), and that carnal unions should not be exhibited as they have no religious connotation. Neither do the Vishnu cults seem to have favoured these stylistic exercises representing the body. If certain of the Khajuraho temples dedicated to Vishnu or to one of his avatars do possess some suggestive sculptures, it is probably because the same sculptors worked on the temples. The reason why erotic decoration features mainly in the Shiva sanctuaries will be explained presently.

WHETHER EROTIC OR NOT, ALL THE SCULPTED BEINGS ON THE TEMPLE
FACADES EMIT AN ENERGY, A LUST FOR LIFE, A POWER AND A GRACE THAT CANNOT LEAVE THE
FAITHFUL UNMOVED. EACH POSITION OF THE BODY OR ANGLE OF THE HEAD,
EACH GESTURE OR MOVEMENT OF THE HANDS HAS A PARTICULAR MEANING. LIKE THESE DANCERS,
IT TELLS THE ETERNAL STORY OF THE GODS.

There are two different styles of sculpture on the Khajuraho temples. The stone was either first carved in the round then affixed to the walls and in the corners with tenon and mortise joints, or sculpted in very high relief on the walls themselves. Isolated sculptures generally feature the divinities to whom the sanctuaries are dedicated or certain animals, either the vahana – mounts of the gods – or animals which represent their avatars. There are other imaginary beings, including a kind of mythical griffin (*shardula*) crushing a woman or man in a symbolic representation of the force of carnal desire. Some of these images, separated from their architectural context, have been placed on the platforms or beneath isolated mandapas.

Even in the Shiva temples, the rooms inside the temples as well as the corridors around the inner sanctuaries are without images of couples of lovers (*mithuna*). On the other hand, the grace of the female body is exhibited in all its aspects, and the sculpture gives full expression to its variety of attitudes. The emphasis is on the suppleness of the bodies, the gracefulness of the poses and their meaning in apparently insignificant, everyday actions such as looking in a mirror, dyeing the sole of a foot, writing a letter or putting on make-up. For the architect as well as for the sculptor, once the devotee has reached the heart of the temple, he must free himself from desire and all its means of satisfaction in order to lose himself in the contemplation of the pure beauty of the divine energies represented by these women or girls, each in a different pose. Here one sees a beautiful girl modestly hiding her embarrassment with her hand or a veil; there another girl appears to be frightened by the antics of a little monkey; there again a celestial beauty (*surasundari*) emerging from her bath, discovers a scorpion on her thigh.

The artists have scrupulously observed the canons of Indian sculpture as first observed in the Satavahana and Rushan periods and followed in the cave paintings of the Gupta period as well as in the temple bas-reliefs and sculpture in general. The forms are full and generous, woman being the obvious symbol of fertility; the attitudes are graceful yet filled with humility and respect, as becomes the Indian woman; the faces impersonal, since the gods' energies are undifferentiated in the absolute; the lower limbs appear neglected, being mere material supports. The female body is thus representative of the whole of creation: emerging from crude matter, it gradually breaks free and culminates in a sort of idealization of the spirit within, whose ascent is embodied in the curves of the spine. The spine, according to the Tantric theories current in India in the Chandella period (and at about the same time in Orissa and some other parts of India), is likened to the serpent of energy (*kundalini*) stretching from the base of the sacrum to the crown of the head and supporting the six stages (*chakra*) of the spiritual evolution which the follower must awaken one after the other in order to transmute his sexual energy (which is life energy) into pure spirituality, thus attaining union with the divine.

> O mother Kundalini ! Coiled
> in the heart of the Muladhara-chakra,
> You waken the universe to existence
> as you rise in a burst of fire
> up to the Sahasrara-chakra,
> where you unite with Shiva.
> (*Tantrasara*)

The serpent of Shiva, which is female, is also likened to Durga, of which it is one of the names. Durga represents the active aspect of Shiva and is supposed to link the energies of Shiva and Vishnu. This explains why there is also an abundance of these female forms in the temples dedicated to Vishnu. The male divinity is in essence passive and, in order to act, he depends upon his female counterpart who represents his active, creative energy. Even though the male divinity (Shiva and Vishnu being among the most important of the Hindu pantheon) possesses in substance every possibility of creation, he cannot act without the aid of the female (*subordinate deities)* who represents his energies (*shakti*). Similarly, the female energies of the divinity could not exist without him; they would be mere bodies without souls.

The sects adoring this shakti as the Great Goddess or as the Mother attribute to her an infinite number of names, such as Devi, Kali, Durga, Ambika, Bhairavi, Ganga, Parvati etc., and invoke her in preference to the male divinity. The *Tantra*, the holy books devoted to her cult, state that the creating consciousness of Shiva draws its power of will from the Revealed, "the original substance still formless and undetermined, but latent, ready to take on all the forms of the divine Desire." (N. Ménant, *Hymnes à la déesse*)

This is the concept behind the erotic sculptures on the outer walls of some of the Khajuraho temples. The shakti is a woman, the matrix which enflames the man's desire to procreate, the latter's nature remaining however unaffected. She is also the *maya*, the illusion which takes on an infinite number of forms in order to make us conscious of existence.

> For I, Shiva, am the sperm
> and the red humour is my shakti:

When these two fuse together
I unite with Her !
Who knows this is fulfilled;
his body becomes a god's !
(*Siva-samhita*, 4,87)

What finer illustration could the artists employed by the Chandella foll-owers of this doctrine have found than the various physical unions described in Vatsyayana's *Kamasutra* ? One chapter of these aphorisms on carnal pleasure composed in the fourth or fifth century describes the multiple ways in which the man-god copulates with the woman-shakti in order to set in motion the forces governing creation and existence.

Most of the Chandella rajahs must have adhered to the Tantric cults of Kaula and Kapalika. According to the texts, the play entitled *Prabodha Chandrodaya* (The Rising Moon of the Intellect) was first performed by its author Krishnamishra at the court of the rajah Kirtivarman.

The Kaula cult placed emphasis on the union of Shiva with his shakti and advocated the most varied sexual practices in order on the one hand to exhaust desire and on the other to awaken the energy serpent, the kundalini. The cult thus allowed the great of this world, who had the leisure for it, to satisfy their inclination for debauchery while at the same time offering a sacrifice (in the religious sense of the word) to the Goddess.

The cult of the Kapalikas was more secret as it involved human sacrifice, and the temple named Chaunshat Yogini may have been one of their altars, though there is nothing to substantiate this assertion. The *Prabodha Chandrodaya* states that the Kapalikas were at that time known by the name of Somasiddhantin, and that one of their beliefs was that they could only attain liberation (*moksha*) by practising all kinds of excess (condemned by the other Hindu faiths), notably sexual intercourse. It is however unlikely that the Kapalikas, although they may have existed at Khajuraho, took any part in the creation of the temples. The people generally held them in very low esteem, while the Kaulika on the contrary were highly respected by great and small alike, the former especially ascribing to them immense powers (*siddhi*).

In the minds of the faithful, the ritual of sexual intercourse gave concrete form to the mystical union of the *lingam* of Shiva penetrating the *yoni* of his partner. All positions were thus permitted, even the most acrobatic and improbable, as different forms of creation. Each act has a specific name originating from the way it is performed. The woman, or nubile girl in the rite of initiation for marriage, is honoured in every imaginable way, for she is the shakti, the potential mother, the one who will give life to existence through union with her husband who, according to Indian custom, must be a god to his wife.

These images with their capacity for stimulating desire have often been interpreted as a deliberate incitement on the part of the Chandellas in order to increase the population and thus the wealth of the kingdom. Philosophers on the other hand have seen in them the concept of individual souls seeking union with the divinity by every possible means, like the large numbers of shepherdesses (*gopi*) gathering to unite with Krishna-Vishnu in the meadows and groves of Vrindavan.

There is certainly no pornographic intention in these representations. Throughout history, Indian philosophy has dictated that the woman is to be revered and that sexual union is the most sacred activity, to be consummated in a religious spirit, whatever manner may be used. The sexual act is considered to be essentially creative, an act of union between the two inseparable principles of the universe. In performing it the man feels equal to the divinity itself, while the woman is also aware of taking part in the great cosmic act of creation. There is no idea of one being subjugated to the other, but rather a profound feeling of equality, of sharing in the accomplishment of a divine task.

The union of the two principles may be achieved on different levels, ranging from sheer bestiality as in the scene on the platform of the Lakshmana depicting intercourse between a man and a mare, through every form of love-making to the pure abstraction of merely suggested coupling. The Kaulika, like the adherents of the Tantric theories and the Shakta (devotees of the Goddess), considered that divine unions could know no limits, unlike earthly ones restricted by the physical capacity of human and animal bodies. Every form of union may be envisaged, at least intellectually; none is expressly forbidden. Certain are however not recommended, for reasons of morality or simply custom. In the *Kamasutra*, Vatsyayana passes over them in silence or, as in the case of fellatio (*auparishtaka*), refers to them as being practised by a particular people.

The gods are neither lewd nor prudish: such notions are human. Their task is to create, destroy and re-create, with no thought of morality or custom, so it would have been irrelevant to try to impose limits on them. Only those determined to see evil can find indecency in these works of pure innocence. One has to have the puritanical, narrow-minded mentality of the first discoverers of Khajuraho to see "monstrosities" there, or to believe, as Percy Brown claimed in his work on Hindu architecture, that the Khajuraho temples had fallen into oblivion because of the "sinister ritual" performed there.

But as we have already pointed out, the sculpted decoration on the temples of this ancient religious city is not restricted to images of celestial women and holy coupling. The sculptors' talents were also applied to subjects we consider more elevated, even though from their point of view all were equally worthy of representation.

The depiction of animals is remarkable both in the observation of their attitudes and in the boldness of stylization, for example Varaha, the gigantic wild boar, representing the third of Vishnu's avatars. Carved in a huge block of stone blackened by the hands of the faithful, it crouches as if to spring before the visitor climbing the steps of the mandapa under which it shelters, in front of the Lakshmana temple. The whole head and body of this extraordinarily stylized sculpture is adorned with 674 small figures of divinities, animals and snakes, the significance of which is not always clear. A statuette of a divinity, perhaps Prithvi, the Earth, which is now broken, was placed between its front paws. Another colossal animal statue representing the white bull of Shiva, Nandin, also sculpted from a single block of sandstone, stands facing the Vishvanatha temple in the western group. Below the porch of a small mandapa, the only vestige of a temple called Mahadeva, on the same platform as the great Kandariya-Mahadeo, a shardula sitting on its hind quarters appears to be attacking a man kneeling under it. This symbol of desires enslaving humanity has been interpreted as an allusion to the Chandella custom which, according to legend, required every prince on reaching the age of 16 to stone a lion to death.

On the upper corners of the roof of the Vishvanatha are a dozen large elephants sculpted in the round, placed on individual projecting bases. Each one is in a different position and either caparisoned with garlands or adorned with bracelets and jewels on the legs. Perched in the sky, they give an impression of complete unreality.

The animalist art becomes more realistic in the bas-reliefs on the sides of the high platforms of the large temples. Here the sculptor has chosen to show parades of horses, elephants, camels and cows, accompanied by groups of dancers and musicians or men in arms. A man is seen holding a dog on a leash, behind another leading a goat. The style is less elaborate than that of the surasundari and the mithuna on the temple walls, but more realistic. The friezes decorating the platforms seem moreover to have been executed either before the temples were built, or at some later period and by less talented artists.

The statues of various divinities adorning the walls of the temples and enthroned in the Holy of Holies are also elegantly worked. They are sometimes exceptionally large in size, as for example the statue of Adinatha, the first of the Jain tirthankara to be found in the restored Shantinatha sanctuary, which is four metres high. Standing naked, in the rigid attitude typical of the tirthankara representations, he is identifiable only by the effigy of a bull which stands at his feet. Under the mandapa roofs are niches placed at regular intervals along the edge of the parallel bands corresponding to the successive corbels, in which are added effigies of divine images, the Dikpala or guardians of the horizons, Indra the East, Yama the South, Varuna the West and Kubera the North, as well as images of intermediary divinities.

Thus, in almost every temple, the essential elements of the Hindu pantheon are honoured. Most of the niches in the mandapa roofs are surmounted by a sort of decorative pediment dominated by the extended arches – *chaitya*, or *kudu* in southern India – in a richly adorned setting studded with human or animal figurines. The corners of the mandapa roofs are also embellished with small-scale urushringa which reproduce the mandapa itself. The porches are embellished on the upper part with multi-foiled arches arising from the mouths of the makara. Delicately chiselled motifs are suspended from these arches, softening the hardness of the technique used in their construction. Inside the mandapas the columns, usually square and massive, support capitals decorated with gana, dwarves crouching in the position of mini-Atlases. The shaft of the columns is engraved with serpentine leaf designs. Some have finely-worked brackets two-thirds of the way up to hold oil lamps. Finally, in the inner corners of the mandapa, at the base of the cupola, figures of surasundari or standing divinities sculpted in the round make the transition between the square at the base of the ceiling and the worked corbelling of the inner dome. This type of figure reappears a century later in the female figures of madanakai decorating the corbels of the Hoysala temples at Mysore. It is also reminiscent of the shalabhanjika (woman-spirit of the trees) of the ancient Hindu and Buddhist structures representing a woman clinging to the branches of a tree with one hand. Here we see an illustration of the perpetuity of Indian sculptural tradition.

All the flat surfaces of the temples are decorated either with plant motifs, horizontal bands with figures, female figures or divinities carved in the round.

Thus the abundance of forms represented seeks to symbolize that of life itself. The profusion of decorative elements and sculptures, no two of which are exactly alike, evokes in the Hindu mind the infinite variety of forms of life in both the divine and human worlds. The temple ultimately takes on a unique significance, becoming a small-scale replica of the entire universe.

Architectural decoration and niches provide an excuse for technical and artistic virtuosity. Here the arches (chaitya) are superposed in honeycombs to form a pediment which supports a squatting dancer at its apex by means of a crouching gana. Each niche holds a separate sculpture or group, women and lovers, or the figure of a divinity, in this case Shiva, recognizable by his trident *PAGES 94-95:* One is overwhelmed by the number and beauty of the sculptures on the outer walls of the Khajuraho temples. It is curious to see how the artists have composed their works, mingling divinities, single or in couples, women at their toilet or wearing the simplest clothes, mythical animals and praying naga.

Femininity, being the symbol of fertility, has always inspired Indian sculptors. Here a beauty with resplendent breasts tries to extract a thorn from the sole of her foot with a sharp instrument (*ABOVE*). *LEFT:* Depicted in every possible and imaginable form by the Khajuraho sculptors, physical love is inseparable from the mother's love for the child. Creation cannot be expressed by duality alone; its ultimate object lies in continuity, represented by the child, the element which joins the two partners, the result of their union. *PAGES 100-101:* In the brilliant afternoon light the frieze on the base of a temple shows cavalry and soldiers armed with lances and headed by a drummer, setting off for war. The movement is lively and the postures varied and supple, once again accentuated by the effect of the sun's rays.

In India, dyeing the soles of the feet is considered essential because henna impedes sweating and forms a necessary part of feminine make-up. The woman in love takes great care of her body in order to please her lover who, when they come together, is both her god and her prey. The perfection of her heavy breasts is filled with the promise of sensual satisfaction for the man-god (*above*). *right:* Indian decoration abhors empty space and every available surface is filled. Here children play or pray at the feet of a divinity; there one sees the recurring theme of the griffin, this time with the beak of a bird of prey, crushing a woman before the impassive eyes of a bearded, mustachioed divinity who wields a sceptre adorned with a skull and holds a bird in his left hand. *pages 104-105:* The sculpture is as sinuous as the plant from which it draws its inspiration. The profusion of couples, gods and dancers conjures up the infinite ramification of branches and leaves of a tree, whose powerful trunk can be regarded as the temple itself.

Although the theme of the couple and the kiss reappears constantly in the decoration of the temples, this is not the passionate embrace of earthly lovers. The impassive expression of the faces shows that this is rather a rite of creation in which both the bodies and souls of the participants are involved.

Tender, protective gestures sculpted in stone portray a gentleness of behaviour, as well as the desire of the faithful for the ultimate bliss of union with the divinity. *PAGES 110-111:* This small female figurine demonstrates the perfect artistry of the sculptors employed by the Chandellas. The young woman's pose is extraordinarily realistic. The suppleness of the body, the delicate movement of the arm and the beauty of the facial features give the impression of a portrait. This softness contrasts curiously with the more stereotyped lines of the divinity whom she seems to be looking at, and a heavenly being plays the flute as if urging them to come together and dance.

In India, femininity has aways been expressed by fullness of the breasts, belly and hips: the promise of fertility, carnal pleasure and perfection. Homage to the body of woman – mother and mistress combined – is also homage to the creative power of the gods. Thus the sculptors have done their utmost to portray the female body as sensually as possible. The jewels adorning it serve only to emphasize the roundness of the curves.

Unlike elsewhere on the temples, the sculptor brings out the elegance of a woman's legs with perfect mastery of line (*above*). *Left:* The passion of this divine embrace is accentuated by the golden light of sunset. The woman stands on tiptoe, a pose rarely depicted in Indian sculpture, as if trying to get closer to the face of the divinity she clasps in her arms.

In a corner of the ceiling of a mandapa, perched on a cornice and supported by a gana, a woman seems to be looking at the decoration. She turns her back on the visitor as if inviting him to follow her to more ethereal heights. The flowing line of the female back appears to have had an erotic force during the Chandella period which it later lost.

ALL THE SENSUALITY, THE TENDERNESS BORN OF DESIRE AND THE COQUETRY WHICH CHARACTER-
IZES THE FEMALE SEX ARE SKILFULLY PORTRAYED BY THE ARTIST IN THIS BEAUTIFUL WOMAN LOOKING
IN A MIRROR AS SHE DOES HER HAIR, OR IN THE SAME WOMAN'S ABANDON WHEN SHE LEAVES HER
MIRROR TO SURRENDER WILLINGLY TO HER LOVER'S CARESSES.

Perhaps nowhere else in the world has such a hymn to the beauty of woman been sung. The sculptor emphasizes the curves of the female body with its infinite flexibility in contortions which, though often daring, appear natural. The gracefulness of the models is also highlighted by the minute detail of their lavish jewelry.

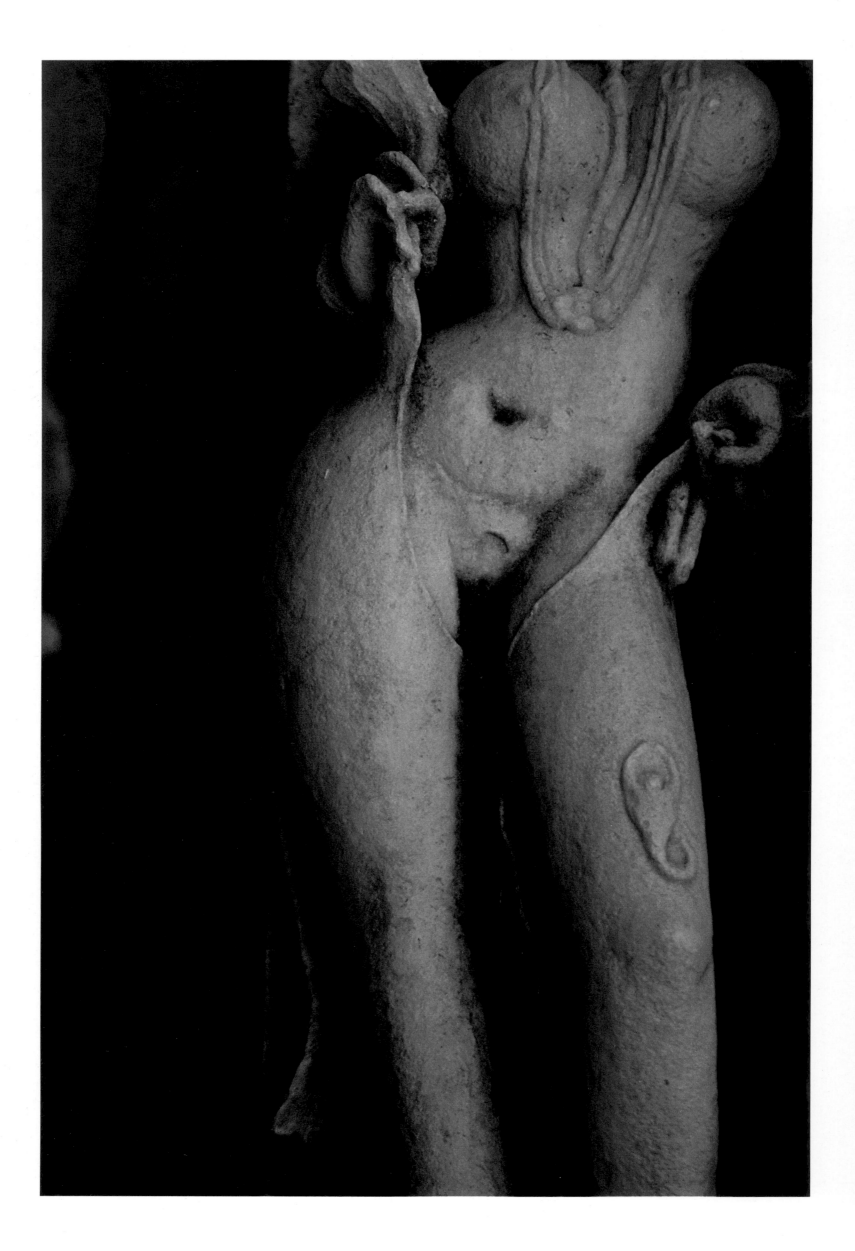

THE WOMAN UNDRESSING OR UNDOING HER BELT IS A FREQUENT THEME IN THE ART OF KHAJURAHO. SOMETIMES A SYMBOL IS ADDED, HERE A SCORPION. IS THE YOUNG WOMAN REMOVING HER CLOTHES BECAUSE SHE IS AFRAID OF THE INSECT, OR DOES IT SYMBOLIZE SOMETHING ELSE IN THE SCULPTOR'S MIND? *PAGES 130-131:* THE IMAGINATION OF THE KHAJURAHO SCULPTORS KNOWS NO BOUNDS IN THE REPRESENTATION AND GLORIFICATION OF THE FEMALE BODY. THE POSES ARE MOST VARIED, BUT THE FULLNESS OF THE CURVES ALWAYS EVOKES THE SOURCE OF LIFE, CREATION AND FERTILITY.

Generous curves, voluptuous abandon, desire, whether shared or refused, ritual copulation: everything serves as a pretext for beauty. Thus, the most unbridled eroticism becomes chaste, the courtesan is a virgin, and the lover is transformed into a high priest singing the praises of love in homage to the gods.

In Indian sculpture the legs have no erotic significance, unlike the rest of the female body. They are therefore treated as mere supports, devoid of any power of suggestion. In the erotic poses they play a secondary role, as if to throw into relief the full, rounded lines of the women's bodies. No sexual position or form of caress with hands or mouths is omitted, for the woman's role is to give pleasure in every possible way, just as the follower of the divinity must satisfy the object of his love with all his strength and soul. In traditional Indian society the husband represents the god to his wife. The lover is idealized in the same way.

Eroticism is present everywhere on the temple walls, sometimes blatant on the plinths, but always subtly suggested on the upper areas. Here, as elsewhere, the couples make love in the presence of secondary characters, but sometimes the sculptor aims to suggest rather than reveal, as in this charming statuette of a woman beginning to undress.

On the walls of the temples there is a curious mixture of apparently contradictory allegories. Here one sees a woman with a child accompanied by other women, there a scene of physical passion in a position reminiscent of a certain chapter of the *Kamasutra*. Yet the child is after all the logical result of such an act.

In ancient India the sexual act was considered to be as natural as eating or drinking, and, like these, it was practised in groups, as the divinity could not be satisfied by a solitary act of creation. The artists therefore represented sexual intercourse between two lovers as a sort of collective rejoicing, with pretty young servants helping the couple to accomplish sometimes acrobatic unions. Both men and women were free to take part in these rejoicings, obviously not indifferent to the act of love which they aided and encouraged. The sculptor depicts this clearly here, while at the same time taking care that the representation of scenes with numerous participants always respects the Indian canons of aesthetics (*above*). *Left*: The subtle interaction of mouldings and sculptures shows that the sculptors worked in close collaboration with the architects. With consummate art, the sculptors made the most of all the possibilities offered by the stone-cutters, as in this example of a woman hiding in a corner of the architecture. The infinite suppleness of the women's bodies comflements perfectly the undulating lines of the engraved decoration on the mouldings.

THE EROTIC ART OF THE KHAJURAHO TEMPLES IS ALWAYS PURE ART RATHER THAN BLATANT EROTI-CISM. THE POSES CHOSEN BY THE SCULPTOR FOR HIS ILLUSTRATIONS ARE NO DOUBT SUGGESTIVE, BUT THEY ARE EXPRESSED WITH A SENSE OF HARMONY OF GESTURE AND BALANCE OF FORM THAT MAKE THEM GLORIOUS AND ETERNAL.

"You are seated on a lotus, Drunk with the lotus perfume, You are free from fear, You take on all the forms of your desire, For the sphere of desire is your realm of action, O liana, entwined around the tree that satiates all desires." (*Mahanirvana Tantra*). *PAGES 152-153:* As at a theatre, every scene should be viewed under particular lighting. Playing with shadows and contrasts, the sun sometimes reveals and sometimes conceals an act, constantly changing the scene, as if to show that nothing is ever static, everything is in a state of evolution and one must therefore not attach more importance to one representation than another.

# LAKSHMANA TEMPLE
## KHAJURAHO

Scale of 5 · · · · 0 · · · · 5 Metres

Scale of 10 5 0 10 20 Feet

LONGITUDINAL SECTION

PLAN AT LEVEL A-Á

PRADAKSHINA

GARBHA-GRIHA · ANTARĀLA · MAHĀ-MANDAPA · MANDAPA · ARDHA-MANDAPA

PRADAKSHINA

N

PLAN AT LEVEL B-B́

# THE MONUMENTS

There is no official list of the Khajuraho monuments. Successive authors have numbered them as they pleased or according to their own itinerary around the site. Listed below simply by name, in alphabetical order, are the most characteristic of the monuments. In addition to these 21 main temples, numerous ruins of temples, decorated wells (such as the Chopra to the north of the site in general) and piles of debris are found scattered in the vicinity. A museum was established in the new village in 1967; it contains very fine sculptures from the destroyed temples. Another small museum, dating from 1910, is situated immediately south of the Kandariya Mahadeo temple.

ADINATHA: Built at the end of the eleventh century, this Jain temple is situated to the southeast of the old village. It has a modern entrance porch and a simple shikhara.

BRAHMA: Actually dedicated to Shiva, this small cruciform structure with granite pillars was built around 900. It is situated to the west of the old village.

CHAUNSAT YOGINI: Probably built at the end of the ninth century, this rectangular platform made of granite is surrounded by small temples (only 35 of the original 65 remain in position). It is located to the southwest of the main western group.

CHATURBHUJA: Also known as Jatkari, this temple dedicated to Vishnu "with the four weapons" is situated south of the village of Jatkari. This temple is exceptional in being open to the west. The mandapa has a splendid circular ceiling. There is a large statue of Vishnu with four arms in the garbha-griha.

*Kandâriya-Mahâdeo*    *Jaïn temple of Adinâtha*

CHITRAGUPTA: Also known as Bharatji, this temple is dedicated to Surya, the sun-god. Situated on a platform northwest of the western group, it has not been well preserved, although the ceiling of the mandapa still has its original decoration.

DEVI JAGADAMBA: Also called the Temple of Kali, it stands just to the south of the Chitragupta, on the same platform as the Mahadeva and the Kandariya Mahadeo. The mandapa has a fine ceiling.

DULADEO: Also called the Kunwar Math. Built at the end of the eleventh

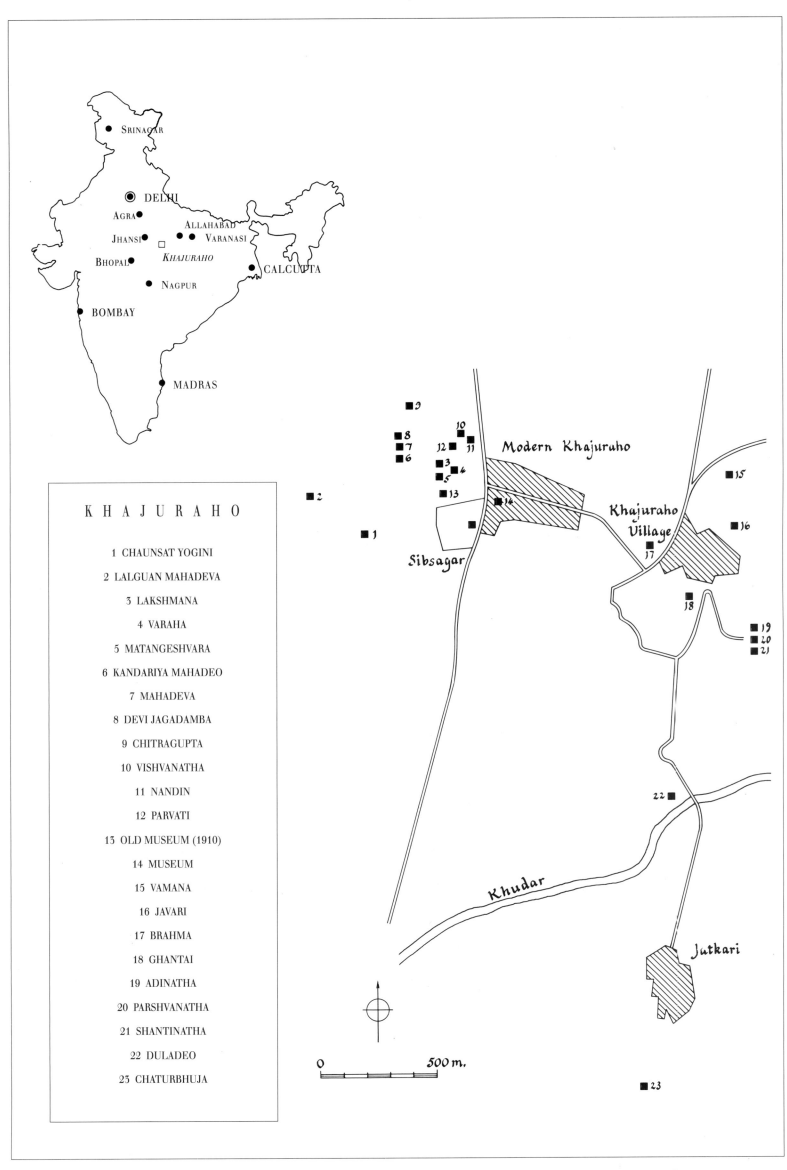

SRINAGAR

DELHI

AGRA
ALLAHABAD
JHANSI
VARANASI
BHOPAL
*Khajuraho*
CALCUTTA

NAGPUR

BOMBAY

MADRAS

**K H A J U R A H O**

1  CHAUNSAT YOGINI

2  LALGUAN MAHADEVA

3  LAKSHMANA

4  VARAHA

5  MATANGESHVARA

6  KANDARIYA MAHADEO

7  MAHADEVA

8  DEVI JAGADAMBA

9  CHITRAGUPTA

10  VISHVANATHA

11  NANDIN

12  PARVATI

13  OLD MUSEUM (1910)

14  MUSEUM

15  VAMANA

16  JAVARI

17  BRAHMA

18  GHANTAI

19  ADINATHA

20  PARSHVANATHA

21  SHANTINATHA

22  DULADEO

23  CHATURBHUJA

Modern Khajuraho

Khajuraho Village

Sibsagar

Khudar

Jutkari

0          500 m.

# BIBLIOGRAPHY

AGARWAL, U. *Khajuraho Sculptures and their Significance*, S. Chand & Co, London 1964

ANAND, M.J. *Kâma Kala, Some Notes on the Philosophical Basis of Hindu Erotic Sculptures*, MARG, vol X, 3, 1957

AUBOYER, J. *La Vie Quotidienne dans l'Inde Ancienne*, Hachette, Paris 1961

— and ZANNAS, G. *Khajuraho*, Mouton, The Hague 1950

BHARATI, A. *The Tantric Tradition*, Rider & Co, London, 1965

BHATTACHARYA, T. *The Canons of Indian Art*, Calcutta 1963

BOSE, N.S. *History of the Chandellas of Jejakabhukti*, K. L. Mukhopadhyay, Calcutta 1956

CHANDRA, M. *The World of the Courtesans*, Vikas, New Delhi 1972

CUNNINGHAM A. *Archaeology of India, Four Reports (1862-63-64-65)*, vol. II, XXII, Khajuraho, Government Central Press, Simla 1871

DEVA, K. *The Temples of Khajuraho in Central India*, "Ancient India", N° 15, 1959
*The Temples of Khajuraho*, 2 VOLS, New Delhi

DENECK, M.M. *La Sculpture Indienne*, Editions Cercle d'Art, Paris 1970

FISCHER, K. *Erotik und Askese in Kult und Kunst des Inder*, Cologne 1979

FLORY, M. *Khajuraho*, Delpire, Paris 1965

FOUCHET, M.P. *L'Art Amoureux des Indes*, Lausanne 1955

FRÉDÉRIC, LOUIS *Dictionnaire de la Civilisation Indienne*, Laffont, Paris 1987
*Inde, Temples et Sculptures*, A.M.G., Paris 1959

GANGULY, D.C. *The Chandellas*, in "The Struggle for Empire," *The History and Culture of Indian People*, Bharata Vidya Bhavan, Bombay 1957, pp. 58-61

GONDA, J. *Les Religions de l'Inde*, vol.II, *L'Hindouisme Récent*, Payot, Paris 1965

GOSWAMY, B.N. *Rasa, Les Neuf Visages de l'Art Indien*, in "Galéries Nationales du Grand Palais", March-June 1986

GOUDRIAAN, T. and GUPTA, S. *Hindu Tantric and Shakta Literature*, Wiesbaden 1981

GUPTA, S. HOENS, D.J., GOUDRIAAN, T. *Hindu Tantrism*, E. J. Brill, Leyde 1979

INDRA *The Status of Women in Ancient India*, Lahore 1940

LAL, K. *Immortal Khajuraho*, Delhi 1967
*The Religion of Love*. Delhi 1971

*MARG*, vol. X, 3, special number on Khajuraho, Bombay June 1957

MEHTA, R.J. *Konarak, The Sun-Temple of Love*, Taraporevala, Bombay

MITRA, S.K. *The Early Rulers of Khajuraho*, Calcutta 1958

PRAKASH, VIDYA *Khajuraho*, Taraporevala, Bombay undated

RAWSON, PH. *L'Art du Tantrisme* (translated by L. Frédéric) A. M G., Paris 1973
*Erotic Art of the East*, New York 1968

SARKAR, G. *Notes on the History of Shikhara Temples*, in *RUPAM* 10, 1922

SRIVASTAVA, B. *Iconography of Shakti*, Varanasi 1978

THOMAS, P. *Kam Katha, Love Themes from Ancient Indian Classics*, Taraporevala, Bombay undated
*Indian Women through the Ages*, London 1964

WOODROFFE, J. *Shakti and Shakta*, Madras 1952

— and AVALON, A. *The Serpent Power*, Derain, Lyons 1959/Madras 1972

ZANNAS, E. *Khajuraho*, Mouton, Gravesend 1960